M000206696

RUST IN AUGUST

RUST IN AUGUST

POEMS

GREG SHAW

WHALER
BOOKS

Buena Vista, VA

Copyright © 2023 by Greg Shaw

All rights reserved, including the right of reproduction
in whole or in part in any form without the
express written permission of the publisher.

1 3 5 7 9 10 8 6 4 2

Library of Congress Control Number: 2023921326

Rust in August
Greg Shaw

p. cm.
1. Poetry: Subjects & Themes—Places
2. Poetry: Subjects & Themes—Animals & Nature
3. Poetry: American—General

I. Shaw, Greg, 1964– II. Title.
ISBN 13: 979-8-9892186-1-5 (softcover : alk. paper)
ISBN 13: 979-8-9892186-2-2 (ebook)

Cover Image by Ryan Russell
Design and Layout by Karen Bowen

Whaler Books
An imprint of
Mariner Media, Inc.
131 West 21st Street
Buena Vista, VA 24416
Tel: 540-264-0021
www.marinermedia.com

Printed in the United States of America

This book is printed on acid-free paper meeting the
requirements of the American Standard for Permanence
of Paper for Printed Library Materials.

Contents

A Window Seat

Numberless, cumulus clouds
    slip past elegant engines loud

Freshly plowed fields of wheat
    greening in shapes shaped neat

Below a deep azure bay
    slips by so far away

Curving brown shorelines
    and twirling wind turbines

Ahead beckons a boulder-beaded beach
    just within eyesight's reach

Turning, I press to the window
    The greatest show on earth is Earth

Center seat, this time

We can see no lights below
But after some turbulence
We are consoled

The honey lights of home
A galaxy of lamps and lanterns

A tiny town, perhaps a county
From seven miles high

No one in my confines looks
They stare at phones
They fawn over Facebook
And watch videos, a motherlode of motherboards

Do they know?
The greatest show on earth
is Earth

Fern Lane

Every summer during these two weeks
    a leafy canopy cools our rented cottage.
I am surrounded by another's books
    ideas from another village
Every new fact fascinates; one connected to the other
    Poems, plays, paintings
A game of cricket or croquet
    Aren't we posh?

Veterans Day

Half past eleven by the time we arrive
A band beckoning
The parade already passing
How many people is hard to derive

The 11th hour, the 11th day, the 11th year.

A celebration just beginning
Muffled applause, a city paused
And then, for a moment, remembrance
"Another time"—fathers and uncles sigh

November grey, warm, and windless, we yearn.

Decorated squads have passed this way
Ballplayers from a nearby Fenn
Patriots who fought for them
Young Americans on a Common they lay

Boom, boom, boom goes the drum.

Yesterday
A garage sale band
Played Star Wars at 4 p.m.
Outside the Cinema Grande

Poom, poom, poom went the horn.

Street musicians—the vagabonds on guitars
An old many on his erhu violin
Played-on, then hushed

To hear the rustle of leaves

Along the Charles

I cannot tell you why the geese do not fear us
Perhaps because they have migrated so far

They shuffle, waddle, saunter, or skip
across this mean strip—this gravelly path
where joggers breeze by
as nannies push strollers and coddle toddlers

The women's brown ears
plugged with matte white airbuds

To listen

Boylston

Hateful howls the wind
    'round alleyways and corner lanes

Sans scarf—no woolen coat, gloveless
    nothing to fight off an insurgence of ice

Head bowed; muscles tight
    your touch still aches, the cold still stings

Metal doors ahead collect me
    Oh, to have froze

Sandcastles on the Cape

A storm of white sheets
Shaded our peach-colored backs
beneath a box fan's breeze
Windows thrown wide exposing, what?

The kids, still young, stop to nuzzle.

For days now the postal clerk in town
has parsed words to warn
of a heat wave not yet seen on apps
or the paper's four-colored maps

And the baseball throwing, the tennis ball hitting
have fallen through
as friends have slipped away
by cover of summer haze

to find early fall in a beige-lit mall

We take the tools of a journeyman beach worker—
Trowels, buckets
SPF-guarded faces and backs

We will build castles, moats, and structures close to the earth
Our sloppy sweat, delusions of architectural prowess

The jelly-speckled waves and the screaming land lovers
Threaten our little sandy Spanish model, a Spanish Toledo

Dug out of the Cape Cod shore
Where the seawater races and deep pools recede

Before lunchtime, away on our porch, we pause to remember
three solitary sandcastles, each fortified, by something

One walled, surrounded by a moat.
One wider, the other more remote.

On Buzzards Bay, the warm sea wind, the sun at right angles
Stirring up silences, sleep, and regrets

We sat on summer couches

The luckiest people on the face of the earth
Our whole lives behind us, our whole lives before us

Tonight the winds blow up white hot thunderheads
and purple cold clouds

Reminders of terror, horror, and splendor
Stretched across the heavens, reflected off Vineyard Sound

Off toward Nobska, from the deck still visible,
three clumps of sand stand, defiant

Blue Jello

At a minimum there are four very small children around us at all times. Sometimes more. This means that there is controversy, dispute, crying, laughing, screams, and screeches at every possible moment. Conversations are rushed if not halted mid-sentence. Dinners start early and invariably run late. The days are a constant compromise between eating, napping, exertion, silent reading, a library, a playground swing. There are meltdowns, bumped heads, and turns taken out of turn. And then there is a brief moment when two tiny cousins find the corner of a deck. They sit down in the way only children do, and the light of an outdoor lamp turns their hair to halos and their bodies into illuminated silhouettes. They are eating blue Jello, and the wisp of an August moon is rising. The soft lick of waves can be heard just over the hedge. And we all laugh contentedly at the beauty of that picturesque moment. Scorched more deeply is the mark it leaves on you and me, on us, where this moment is simpler, softer, more magic than the sum total of every other moment before it.

Baseball

I can count on one hand
The number of times you have played this game
Without me standing there near the diamond
Quietly watching, never wandering.

I read once that Ichiro's dad, like Tiger's, stood long hours
never missing a swing.

Even when I coach the others or stand in as impartial umpire
I catch myself stealing a glance—
Your bended-knee snag, the full-chested heave
And the way you may feel running into position.

How could a dad miss this?

There is blinding sun and there is dust caught up
in this wind and withering words, the missed call
and the coaching blunder. It can hurt and it can heal.
Baseball is a metaphor

for nothing

One great and glancing blow
Words are felled like timber

Sailboats

Barefoot I stepped out onto the deck
On an airy June evening

To straighten wind-strewn placemats
Pillows blown to the ground

Looking up from my tidying, a bruised purple sky
Dips down into an unwarm lake

And, oh, look a sailboat regatta
It's boating's opening day

But look again, those brilliant white sails
Are not sails at all

But tulips in a neighbor's yard
Positioned just so

Neighbors

In the driveway, she caught my eye
pausing to hush her Bluetooth call

Not so tall, three white dogs tugged on leashes
I set down the trash

As we do.

"Those trees in the yard are blocking our view"
Will you help us pay to cut them down?"

What little she knew. My name being Shaw,
Scotts-Irish for a grove of trees

No, we will not help.

Thanksgiving

From my window, warm inside
    A lonely street in fall I spied
a curious scene, what might be in store?

Solitary he sweeps
    Away fallen leaves
into the street, downwind from his door

Perhaps he fears someone will slip
    When guests come for turkey and parsnip
or will no one come to share his festive hour

The broom in his hand he sets aside with a knee
    Reaching into his pocket he fiddles for a key
Above him, twirls a vine once thick with flowers

Ode to Kehinde Wiley's
"Rumors of War"

I took a room on 10th Avenue
to be near, to witness
a majestic statue's final days in New York City

Atop his pedestal, a resistant young man
astride a powerful steed
silhouetted and sanctified by neon, in Times Square.

Kehinde formed this statue
Now it redirects a path for us beneath

The rumors of war—they are rumors no more
They surround and suffocate

On the statue's stoop, I sit with a cigarette-smoking
        Spiderman
Still costumed after posing for Instagram

All around giant LED screens, the city's sirens
The sounds of slurring voices
Heads hovering over smartphones

Your silence resounds.

The cranes are coming
to remove you to Virginia

Tonight the city's snow stains your shoulders,
and the "good" people on both sides

Look up: an ad's half-clothed model, "queen of holiday
    parties"
Listen: the haunting whisper of a coy passerby, "cocaine?"

It's the wee hours now, the cranes are coming
To remove you to Virginia

To take you to Richmond
To take you to Richmond

See that you are not troubled

Removal crews have arrived
The machinery is in place.

Your rebellious gaze looks West
Over proud shoulders, a warrior's pose

In New York you welcomed shoppers
In Richmond, Lee and Traveller

Auden asks us to consider Henry James,
who upon observing Monument Avenue
wrote of melancholy, a bereft image, an infelicitous look

Tomorrow you decamp, South
Past capitols, the Mason-Dixon
Charlottesville and The Wilderness

Which is more welcoming, Times Square or where you ride?
Which is more prepared—horse or rider?

Say *your* name.

Are you seething or are you seeking?
Are you preaching or are you teaching?

for all these things must come to pass

Like Lee's lieutenants you've left before dawn
for Richmond—Virginia.

But the end is not yet

Venice

The campo divides shade by light
dolce, andiamo, piano
on one side the air is sweet and cooling
the other, intense and withering
pigeons strut, imitating tourists,
then soar, they explore
like all of us

The Tulsa World

How unexpected the persistent roar
Interrupting an otherwise pleasant sleep
Gradually it becomes dad's mower
My window shaded from summer's glow

How to reconcile these sounds with the
thump-thump-thump of a lonely, broken road
when we fled, seeking shelter

I am small in what was dad's guest room
For now it is mine, mattress, closet, and a chest

Awake now my feet and calves remind me
of yesterday's cross-county race on browning fields.
Never the decorated victor
my singlet shaded gold and midnight black

The sports page beckons from the concrete driveway

In a subdivision of a subdivision in a town in a county
Yesterday's race results in agate type

Yoga in Cordoba

The citrus air
Circulates sweetness
softly then suddenly.

Breathe, and walk
or hop
into your downward dog

Blue flower buds
bob and sway
beside blossoms
of lemon and orange
beneath a blanket
of software white clouds

This sunny day
Sink your body
into the floor

A gushing waterfall
replenishes and refreshes
The deep, cold pool
where minnows play
and giants dream.

Reach to the sky

Medieval towers
stand guard to protect
los caballos e iglesia pequeña
And to contain the joy
Lest it slips away
Past *las sierras*

Our warrior pose

Purple Robe

One blowy wintery night
I awoke alert with fright
Smoke tends to trigger the amygdala
Like a threatening sound or a tarantula

Cold I wandered the floors
Snuffling and snorting aloud
What could it be? I searched spastic
The smell conjured burning plastic

Days passed, I'm still perplexed
Could it be a short in the circuits?

Nights became days, the temperatures fell
Without your warmth I longed to be held

At night blankets can freeze
Without heat my comfort ceased
And the distance between us
Presses down with every gust

Tonight, the windows black, the air frigid
Puppy drops to the floor, the darkness persistent
I wander to our closet
Finding your purple robe, I lift it

To wrap the dog in a cloud of your scent
Outside the moon creates a glint
Of hope and the possibility of warmth
All because you can be here, there, both

February

It was a bleak midwinter
Growing old made it harder
But early this morning
We could hear the first bird sing

The flickers have begun their beak-banging
On rooftop chimneys where tin is overhanging

And the room warms sooner
Beneath a sun golden as the finch

If a rainbow reminds us of God's promise
The Camilla's blossoms are His guarantee

Little green leaves sprout like flags in the wind

The heather is no longer lonely
The moss seems more mossy

In February temperatures begin to rise
And there is a smile in our eyes

Translucent insects spiral ever higher

Sunrise

From our tangled warmth in splendid darkness
    My mind geo-caches

Searching for cold harbors and deserted docks
    my mind scanning, surfing

An empathetic forest imagines us, absorbing everything
    spoken or not from the nethermost sediment

Beneath what: a house, a life?
    Does this sentiment crouch below or hover above

One window, eavesdropping, changes black to gray
    There it is.

The Brigadoon Apartments

Our little start-up consisted of three:
mother, brother, and me

A small family who no one seemed to see
We needed an angel, a venture capitalist at least

What do we miss by not investing
in people like this?

At first we drank milk cut by water
to make the carton go that much farther

I had a closet, and removed everything
It would be my new forester office
I wanted to be a forester
And I filled it with books and maps
I measured the trees
I wanted to go far away

One night DR came to visit
He brought his son
My brother and I liked his son
And that kept us out of the way

Sometimes the running water
Didn't run
So I bathed in the swimming pool
not presentable for school

On doorbelling and democracy

At 39 Mad River there live two
their lovely home nestled among cedars blue

Road salt-splattered papers
tucked into my folder
tell me she is old, he is older

I am told to inquire, should they dane to respond,
will you vote for Clarissa or possibly John

Frost's census-taker wandered
rural roads in these White Mountains
to count American people.
Democracy requires many footsteps.

In those same woods, I am the canvasser
cap flaps flopped over both ears
knocking doors for president
a clipboard and pen poised to report

Crunching through last night's snow
I approach their side door
Holding my breath
To hear signs of life

Someone's coming
Maybe a vote
Or an offer to come in
Only for a moment

"I'll go to the poll."
That's all she reveals
And that's ok
My footprints can no longer be seen

Junco

The library door of my daylight rambler
Was left open one winter's day

A Junco skipped to the edge of the entrance
And I snapped my fingers to halt his path

Imagining myself chasing him round the house
with a fitted bedsheet and broom

Blink

Did I learn this from my grandfather the veteran
or my quiet Comanche friend
    To see through a thicket,
    find a pinpoint of light

There's always a glimmer—never look away

Till that light blinks
    Quick, look, that shadow
    will soon step into sight

Ode to the Oud

Today's newspaper, manufactured from wood,
published the obituary of a man who played the Oud

He once picked the strings of this pear-shaped lyre
with fingertips tough like the husk of a nut

Could it be that within his soul it seldom rains
On vinyl I hear his gorgeous refrain

> Hungry, alone, the burn of cold, no sleep.
> Thirst then fear, aching from here to there

> Hope and light and a cool breeze
> Dates and figs and tea gently sweet

this is the sound I hear
when he plays

Strings strain eastward
Buried in deep vibrations, the story of all stories

A tone so beautiful
culled from our pasts
stills the heart, steals our breath

Persia's *barbat* with no frets
Oud is the sound of burning wood

Fading

Down there on the street, voices mutter uncertainty
their sounds softened by apple blossoms
those passersby speaking of something other than happiness
they tote paper bags overflowing with stuff
something like the scent of too much floats over the Irises

Up here, on our perch above the vanishing point,
you and I look westward toward tomorrow
and its piddling rain and its puddling dawn
grayness that can last all day
They cannot see or hear us.

A Star on Top

I,
no, you,
both, all of
us must Love
one another as we
are taught to do so
We.

Oscillations

Ringing in my ear
It drowns out
It competes with
It tells me
It sounds like
It reminds me
It just is

This ruckus of spirits
Those long ago parties
That banging of whispers
The way it was

On the difference between sympathy and empathy

In a songbird, what is it we hear?
    What do we see?
    Imagine on that branch a warbler appears

Using empathy what do we foresee?
    I'd hunt for seed when hungry
    and water when I thirst

Sympathy is the older word but simpler to achieve
    To no longer see songbirds I grieve
    with empathy I can only imagine

Smoking a Pipe at Lake Alice in the Cascade Foothills

Sitting, contemplating the owly woods
I summon Thoreau who at Walden
Turned to the economy of nature
So I ask him directly
"If nature is precious, how do we value it?"
Milton or Marx?

The lacey green shrubs
and towering tree canopies
spirits and mystery
the money and politics of a forest
I am left alone with God
And it's dark now, my pipe still warm
in the chest pocket pressed
against this imperfect heart

The Red River Valley

On the pickup truck radio

Paul Harvey is telling a story
as a ruby cloud of dust
flames up behind us

on that strip steak of a road
charred on both sides
pink down the middle

whilst granddaddy smokes.

Seldom speaking,
he flicks ashes
toward a herd of heifers

Bowed heads, grazing
In tall grasses
Beneath a stand of cottonwood

Tomorrow will be similar
lest it rains and we read all day
or breakfast at the cattle auction

I pray for *Reader's Digest* on worn out couches

Either way, this road crosses a culvert,
a bridge to the other side
not just a conduit but a way back home

Chair

Look no further than your chair
   le sphinx, la silla
Like a cartoon caption contest
   what is it thinking?
What do you want—arms turned upward in plea
   Like Oliver raising an empty cup
Or an arrogant intellectual
   a grim-faced professor awaiting a response
Chairs can be valiant, four stout legs
   Chairs can be otherwise able, three legs or a single peg
I have sat in some with no backbone
   and others stoically upright
Still others recline
   their cushions murmur discernment
Arms of chairs can welcome or entrap
   Do they give rest or sedate?
Is their relationship with the floor
   or objects nearby, like brooms for a chore?
You and your kin are positioned in
   Every room of this house
Inviting the tired, those in need of conversation
   Your welcoming lap invites thin and fat
Fatigued, the loitering louse.

Glaring at my chair

Are you sick or silent?
I just ask because

Beneath you lie both dirt and hope
I think we call that dust bunnies

They will be swept up into a dust bin
Studied and admired

They look like cottonwood seeds
Or even more like dreams

that died several days ago.

The Snoqualmie

Solid stands my split-rail fence
against all harms
Three rails clasped together by
Vertical standing beams
Bark-stripped, knotty with open arms
Protect me from unseen dreams

Birdsong serenades this porch,
calling from the hollow
Depths of yonder firs
A lightning storm to follow.

The blackbird's calling fades
nothing in the woods stirs

Between the branches, a flicker like film
Shadows of people pass as they go
Hikers or specters from a tribe on a march so grim
The last one turns—the wind ceases to blow

Suddenly they are gone and the rain trickles away
Sunshine brightens this emerald forest; birds again sing.
My sturdy fence stands guard, and I determine to stay
to see what riddles the forest tomorrow morning brings.

Whitman lives

In late spring
hours before summer's heat
the air is sweet
in the dooryard,
remembering
lilacs
blooming
still

Softly the wind
recalls a friend
and better angels,
guiding
us
blooming
still

Intermittent Rain

From one section of the eaves
On one slope of the roof
Rain gushes and heaves
Creating silvery sheets

Mirror-like
A reflection
I see me
A boy again

The August wheat ripe
And there is grandma
Wearing a summer dress
Of blue cotton

When the liquid curtain lifts,
The rain intermittent,
soaring soaked clouds
pause and pass
        over now
the deluge, its unrepentant rivers

Lanes of Destruction

Screaming runs the asphalt street where mastodons of mechanical acceleration and left-right turn signals point thither and yon, causing all of us to step quickly to avoid the flaring dawn in which the petrol-pushing titans maximize the depths of their profit moats till money materializes in such amounts that the forgiveness of philanthropy emerges for purposes of preventing a planet too warm, these captains of intellectual property morph into mouthpieces for new modes of transport—no, not just yet—in a little while; right now just speed past pedestrians saluting them all with floods of muddied milkshakes of sludge that will melt into rusty drains racing to rivers that sprint to the sea and vaporize into the beauty of clouds blown back onto meadows of newly planted wheat and forests of fruits so sweet they conceal the hidden toxins we build, or rather tolerate the pursuit of happiness which is little more than convenience and extravagance fulminating intransigence and belligerence from which we are left only to howl.

A Letter to Charlie Soap

My dear friend, Charlie Soap, an exalted name—in English it rhymes with hope, like New Echota and inchoate. Do you remember years ago we sat in a rented car in Century City, California, with Wes Studi soliciting a script about Cherokees, the tribe with a vibe to build waterlines, simple goddam waterlines that no government would build no matter how much and no matter how long? They would not build them because they were just for Indians in Oklahoma's silent settlements like Stilwell and Bell, Briggs and Greasy, Rocky Mountain and Cherry Tree, Piney, Zion, Bunch, Chewey, and Watts where only *tsa-la-gi* is spoken. After all, they are their own nation; so why help after 150 years without running water? The ignorant tried to stop your community development, but Chiefs Mankiller and Swimmer—their names rhyme with overcomer—were having nothing of this. They fought and they overcame. And Charlie this would become your movie: *a-ma*: The Cherokee Word for Water—but unless Johnny Depp played Wilma there was not a chance for Paramount, Disney, or Fox. No one cares, but those who do know what to do don't really know what to do, after all grave promises were gravely broken, so why trust the *yonega*? Those who do know Hollywood and know the BIA, they know about the multibillion dollar lie—we care but we don't—lies that lay like the fly on horse hides, like a sty. They suck the life.

The Interstate

America sprawls
Soaring and sinking
Winding and undulating
From sea to stinking sea
Wealthy and wasted
Dense and deserted
Sliced like a piece
Of angel food cake
By serrated turnpikes
Built by Ike
Three time zones—
Yesterday, today, and forever—
In that order
Hours and days
Interrupted by
Beckoning casbahs
Offering rest
Promising shelter
Surrounded by oaks
Someone planted long ago
Where locusts sing
Above wayside exhibits
So few of us ever read
Because the road is ahead
Always onward
The road most travelled
Rested, it is time to resume

Unconditional

My mountainous oak stares down
Blasts of southerly winds
green leaves rustle, twigs tickled.
In winter, snow lays heavily
on north-facing limbs.
It does not matter.
Trees go with the breeze.

Grandaddy

His farm is sectioned into quarters.
The southeast acres,
so close they could tap on our window

There, at the dusty corner of nowhere
One road north, another road east

You are gone now.

In January fields dark,
by April green,
in June bursting wheat
Lonely, begging—rust in August

There is work to be done.

The crushing weight of generations
Fall on your shoulders
Like one grain underneath a heavy silo
Impossible to breathe, or dream

Its weight falls on us all, now

The Lodge at Lake Crescent in The Olympic Mountains

Thick with aging, not yet elderly
Thinning hair
Their approaching giggles sound close
Through vacuous alpine air

"Olly Olly all come free"
Or is it *alle alle auch sind frei*
One gently corrects the other
On their way walking here

We are not much younger
Would we have played this game?
When we were kids
Will they invite us to play?

Evening is near
End of summer
Eaves fill with scarlet leaves
Endless games of hide and seek

On Mom's Sept 23rd Birthday

When the movies begin
in my head I can sleep
I pray the Lord my soul to keep.

A small computer in my congenital chest
lest the heart suddenly forsake
If I should die before I wake.

What happened to you,
was there a mistake?
I pray the Lord my soul to take.

Turning in

And then when suddenly I slept
The cool and the quiet
Your warmth, our breath
Stories and scenes rich and strange
I dreamt

Was the slumber real
The blue and the gold
And this curious red
Not blood nor a maple in fall

I thought, or thought that I thought

There are dreams and there are dreams
    I said over and over

And then when suddenly I slept
Circling honeysuckle above us stretched
Reaching past the roof into the red buds
Like music carrying hopes for our love

The clouds did weep
Hearing such desire
Notes soaked in the marrow of lives
Lived together for better or worse

Zenith

A butterfly danced in the bright
sunlight to strains of Chopin
played from a transistor radio
near a window left open,
to gather sea breezes

The Middle Fork of the Snoqualmie

On the bright grey boulders below where the deluge
    pours into a deep fast pool near Tanner Road
Throw my ashes there and visit me in June on Opening
    Day when the river beckons for fishers of cutthroat,
    rainbow, and cutbow
You know
The wind whips through the canyon to Mount Si,
as I turn every which way to cast where I like

Pastoral

Ruralis, we miss you more
than perhaps you miss us.
Urbanus bursts at its seams
Uranus has a passing interest
Oreiades pines for the sky

Rural, you are out there
Urban, you are right here
Plural is what compounds wealth
Fertile fields and luxury malls.
You are not black or white

    not everything can
    grow in every place

Another poem about birds (and trees)

If you will

What's so wrong
    with poems about birds

and trees

and looking at a photo of my kids
the reflection of my unruly grey hair
    on the iPhone glass

Sorry. No, not sorry

I like shrubs
and grub worms

rain that falls so fast it looks like metal,
a mirror
I can see myself in

Not every poem is about your horrors

We all see them.

Street Scene

His shadow
stretches West
in that
sliver of sunshine
coffee and cigarette
blowing each nostril into the gutter.

There were fights in the night
bellowing awoke me
nine floors up
rough sleepers
what would Jesus do?
Or even just us

Now
warmth reaches down
his shadow
grows
the height
of towering towers.

Standing on a Bridge in Greenwich, Connecticut

Wealth flows
in cars and trucks
across this tiny tidal waterway
in old
Cos Cob and Riverside

Streetlights guide
Elegant SUVs and sedans
Then take a break
To attack
The silvery surface
Of the darkening water

Oak willows wave
In the humid wind
round road signs
screaming
they seem to say
"Welcome"
They don't mean it

Across this bridge
is a gaunt man
Down below
On slippery rocks
with fishing tackle

We both see minnows playing
Me from up here
And he from down there
Baitfish mid-stream
weaving
watery webs
to elude
what's deeper.
Here are the fish,
They tell us

On the other side
Silent sulking yachts
And colonial manors
with soothing yellow lights
in tiny windows

The sound is blaring
deafening
listen
to the sound
The volume is turned up to 11

I cannot look away

Saturday morning

another playground
    in the woods

chalk stick figures
    on the ground

parents on phones
    playing the same games

over there dark firs
    and skinny pines

they wave to me.
    Not them, me

they want something from me
    I want to give something to them

so I do
    Pinecones dot the field

and three shades of chalk sticks
    forgotten on the sidewalk

a long slender cone I color pink
    Another lime green

the largest now brilliant gold like the sun
    Kids run to place them

like PAAS-dyed Easter eggs here and there
    A trail into the forest.

Leaf Blowers

From the sound of things
We are at war with the leaves.

They point and blast blowers

Battery-powered
Gas-fueled

curbs and corners
Blowers blow and blow

Blare and blow
All summer long

Organic debris
Summer heat

Machines howling
On this lawn and that

Pausing, one man points
the blower to his sweat-stained back

He doesn't hate leaves.
He envies them.

Arbor Day 1

All summer
the husks grew
into round spikes
yellow-green
like *limones*
like prickly pears
That by early fall
promptly fell
splitting open,
fleshy insides
like gaping mouths
of baby birds.

That's when
brilliant afternoon sun
reflected from
an old man's
wide face
onto mine
unexpected joy
to watch him gather
Chinese Chestnuts
with children
in the school yard.

Arbor Day 2

In the park near home
    every day is Arbor Day
        This started before the internet
        in 1994 and
        every April since
    This latticework of trees, vines, and climbing shrubs

Think of the pride
    farmers feel
    Standing in rows
        of produce they've grown

Forester's boots sinking slowly
    Into ground they seed

I dream of that
    Walking briskly
        terra firma,
            Never sauntering

We could be more like the earth
    Inviting, welcoming, rewarding
    To things that grow

The sprawling Chinese chestnut
    Brings joy to fall

Beneath its sweet canopy
    The giant Catawba is an oxygen bar with fragrant
    flowers in late summer, long verdant beans dangle
    down searching for soil

The fern-like leaves of the fig
    Asian pears, crabapples, and cherries

What is Greek for
Love of trees
when filial, agape
and eros fail?
When only Virgil's words
whisper through
the forest dark

Christmas in Hawaii

In the beginning
On Poi'pu Bay
An umbrella tree
Reached for the sky

Taller than hibiscus flowers
Smaller than soaring palms
Bamboo and beauty abound
But lonely was our umbrella tree

It's slender leaves
Project photosynthesis
Sheltering a hidden village
of tropical birds, bugs, lizards
And a feral cat

Still the tree had more to give
And so one night
A leaf was set free
Twirling on a breeze
To the garden below

Browning and yellowing
A leaf in Eden's grasses
A leaf on dark earth
Where the presence of
Metamorphosis
made the leaf a feather
Rising on the wing of an eagle
And the umbrella tree said
It was good, and it was good.

And so it let sail
A few more leaves
Which the trade winds seized
And set down in the sea
Among a school of fish
Silhouettes similar to that
of an umbrella tree leaf.

And so it was.

No fly-fishing

A caviar-colored
Blacktop stream
Meanders
The meridian of
Commonwealth Ave.

In October
spiraling stone flies
warm themselves
in the last light
big fish lurk here

Town and Country

I crush out a cigarette
and look down
on the red bricks below
    Here, a spent apple sauce
    There, a spent tea bag

Girls in tight jeans
and boys looking mean
on the red bricks below
    She plugs the meter
    He paces nearby

We steep in this city

Last night I flicked
stink bugs from
our screened porch
    with no one around
    only mountain air

I crush out a cigarette

President Andrew Jackson, Sequoyah, Chief Justice Marshall, and Some Other Guys Get Into an Argument at the Smithsonian*

I wandered into an argument today at the Smithsonian Museum of American Art. Awkward. The exhibit is entitled, *Out of Many, One.* IKR? Reading the room quickly, as I do, the Cherokee Sequoyah was looking suspiciously to his right, holding up a tablet with his syllabary as if teaching a lesson. The others froze in stoic pose. One was President Andrew Jackson who stood cavalierly in the middle of the room facing Supreme Court Justice John Marshall and his Indian affairs superintendent Thomas L. McKenney, both of whom huddled sheepishly in a corner, to Sequoyah's right. For those who may not remember, Jackson ordered Sequoyah's tribe to leave their farms in the southeast for something euphemistically called Indian Territory. Hell might have been more transparent because many deaths ensued, followed by prolonged oppression. Directly across from Jackson was old Thomas McKenney, who saw fit to commission a portrait of Sequoyah (because Sequoyah was a frigging genius who invented a way to write in Cherokee). McKenney helped his boss, President Jackson, pass the Indian Removal Act of 1830. That's the one that led to the

Trail of Tears. Close by, Chief Justice John Marshall told them both, in one of his historic rulings, that the removal of Indian people from their homelands was unconstitutional. Jackson didn't really care, or listen. McKenney retired. So, yeah, the argument didn't end well.

*Artists on display
- Sequoyah painted by Henry Inman based on an original portrait by Charles Bird King
- Thomas L. McKenney was the founding superintendent of Indian affairs (1824–30). He commissioned the Bird King portrait of Sequoyah and other Native American diplomats but also worked to secure the passage of the Indian Removal Act in 1830 that led to the Trail of Tears
- John Marshall by Cephas Thompson who ruled President Jackson's Indian Removal Act was unconstitutional
- Andrew Jackson, cast by sculptor Clark Mills

What's wrong with me?

We sit here together
But I am not here.
I am elsewhere

Our pulses sync
Sink into the sofa
And the silence surrounds

Both of us
Even when I am here
I'm not here...

Was the mockingbird always there?
Or was it a downy woodpecker?
Did the cardinal's red always set our yard ablaze?

Go fetch your tea.
I'll follow you
Past an open window

Where I see a cloud
The shape of a rickety bus
That carried us once to the shore

The National Portrait Gallery,
District of Columbia

500th block of 7th Street NW
He took off his shoes but
left his hood on

A dark tranquil face
The obverse of midday sun

He was looking toward 7th Street

"Thank god for compound sentences."

With elegance he spoke
And lit an American Spirit

On a half-moon marble bench
Opposite me

We both looked toward 7th Street

"There is something out there, but it's not COVID."

He'd come all the way from L'Enfant
Where he'd gone to order food.

He was prepared for the summer.
He told me so

We heard music coming from 7th Street
"It's a bad word, but it's not war."

An iridescent songbird
He happened to land here

His song pitched to no one
I sat still, only to listen

And we looked toward 7th Street

200th block of 7th Street NW

How great thou art
softly caressed the National Archives building
Coloring 7th Street in its sepia tones
The patina of his trumpet soaked up the sun
That fell upon his bended knees
Where he read scripture from a tattered Bible
To himself and to the tourists passing by

300th block of 7th Street NW

Within the tiny bus shelter
A man, head-bowed man, counted off
Nine steps across
Four steps deep

Not once, but over
And over and over
In the confines of his kiosk
Just a block from Judiciary Square

800th block of 7th Street NW

John sells the homeless newspaper
Across from Walgreens
Across from those strung out
Among the sports fans in home team jerseys
His gray eyes look through and past them

But not through mine
We nod
Knowing well the news already

400th block of 7th Street NW

Cross-legged like a street prophet
Beard long and gaze still longer
Enunciating words never spoken
Inventing new languages
Speaking in tongues
of fire

700th block of 7th Street NW

The soaring rust statue
of the slim silhouette
a man griping a briefcase
and wearing a fedora
Sees everything both ways

Pictures at an Exhibition

These street portraits mingle
with memories of Union militias that marched
through the old hay market, now gone,
Past still-standing gables and makeshift hospitals
Ornate apses and arches and balconets
Just a few blocks from Ford's Theater

The American drama
endures

Ode to a Home One

At the end of a hidden trail
that leads out back
our lab, 'Rillo, is running, frozen in time
beneath swooping purple pillows
of cloud-crusted skies
Our home
His headlong pursuit
of a roundish ball or a tattered toy
where the earth falls away
down the sloping side
of Clyde Hill.

Now the dogs are buried out back
where the smell of mulch
converses with flowerless rhoddies
and banana-shaped pine needles
as a shrike strikes noon
on the shiny tin chimney
the rise over run
of an old, old roof
that once leaked its gushing gutters
into the grated French drains that lead
to the lake.

Ode to a Home Two

Long-gone McKinstry built our house
Near the top of a hill called Clyde

Wee rooms we made bigger
By collapsing walls to make spaces larger

And ceilings raised higher
To make our spirits lighter

Babies, grew into precocious kids, then adults
Who progressed from room to room

Until they were gone
And then we left, too

Leaving the dogs-scratched floor
And the height-notched door

They are silent now
The wood creaks no more

All our pups are buried in the back
Beneath Asian pears and Rainier cherries

Where the fir trees and cedars
used to be.

Backing out of our driveway,
we cried the last time we left

Remembering where we drew life
with pastel-colored chalks

Before the rains came.

Passing Through

On the northbound train
Sit on the right-hand side
On the window

The southeast sunshine
Is never so bright as in winter
Brilliant on my brow

With a salute I shade my eyes
The blurring scenery sharpens
to ponder landscapes unchanged

There is power in a forest
And usefulness in a field
We pause for a passing freighter

Coffee notes from the café car

To my left are people sleeping
Perhaps dreaming of what I see
Through this window

Cracks in the heavens

Twilight beckons, a crimson sun falls.
There and over there, flashes of fireflies
Like the taillights of aeroplanes
soaring over Shenandoah
leaving silky trails of jet spray
Lit up against the pale blue screen we call the sky
Curving in pink like a bony spine

A shine to astonish this stroller, who pauses here
among oaks and gawking deer
to recall the x-rays when together we were unalone
though too often we were alone
when I was that business traveler
up there in 2A, spreadsheets and Syrah
wishing I were here at home.

Caress

Heat drains my soul
White hot here
cool purple over there
On House Mountain

Here I work up a sweat
Attending to other things.

When breezes pick up
Trees and grasses start to dance
Temperatures drop
Thunder roars

Standing in my field
Near large round bails of spring hay

A raindrop like lightning
Jolts the little hairs on my forearms
Another and then another
It tickles, and strokes

This is what a thunderstorm feels like.

Paint Splatters

At the Museo Reina Sofia
Where Picasso's *Guernica* lives
And Juan Gris and Joan Miro sing
I wander the long shallow steps of
An internal staircase
Spiraling up and down through the ages

Who knows when
But an anonymous painter
Dribbled blue paint
from cans he carried in both hands
From *planta tres* down to *la tierra*
The paint speckles circle outward
On the turns and inward
on the descent or was it the ascent?

Midway the paint splatters crisscross
the painter changed hands, perhaps
I studied this work more closely than others
Appreciating the worker's efforts
And the mark left behind.

Chicago, the fever dream

I crossed Michigan Ave.
On my way to the Art Institute
It looked cooler on the other side
In the park's shade

It was a summer's day
An Indian Summer,
I thought to myself

When I saw an Indigenous man
In buckskins and a dangling feather
Resting beneath a tree

He looked at me
I paused
Time froze

He told me he was Black Hawk
"Like the hockey team," I said
What is that?
"It's a sport like lacrosse."
Is it played in the Indian summer?

It is not, it is played on ice in the winter
He looked into the distance
Down Michigan Ave.
Toward the art museum

Pool Spider

At the edge
of a saltwater pool
a spider skates
on surface smooth
out into the depths.
The safety of one shore
slips past, the far one
still out of sight.
The spidery race pauses
Stops, in fact,
in the middle.
Has it succumbed
to the wet?

Boris (I name it) entwines me
as I eye the remaining distance
as its strokes resume
faster, but shorter
quicker and quieter now
the distant shore nearer,
drifting it rests.
I dream of its arrival
on the turquoise tile so close
Boris, lifts its black body
from the dimpled liquid
droplets dripping
and death, not yet.

The Enigma of Arrival

These old barns and farmhouses
Comfort me with their charm
Graying, chipping paint
A rough-hewn, hand-sewn place

Ghosts play in the springhouse
Drawing water from another time

Pokeberry, oak, hickory, and pine
Line the banks of the Maury
Flowing east at the pace
Of a rebel's retreat, when all's over

Stagnant for stretches
Turning turbulent,
like Virginia, at times.

Cy Twombly called this place home,
his "Chitlin' Switch," when not in Rome
V. S. Naipaul writes of ruin and dereliction,
of half-neglected estates.

But on my walks, I find delicious the decay,
the stillness of generations

I no longer long for the city, its symmetry
ersatz ponds, the young and the younger
I love the ivy-eaten tree, and the fallen stone walls
The jagged scratch pines and the old folks.

The Samara of Mount Cuba

We've seen the winged seedpods
swirling and twirling
nature's marriage of maple and wind

dispersing tomorrow's summer shade

But can you see it as a sculptor has?
The samara with scalloped sails
and a minnow's head
and a midsection like the body
of a paper plane pinched
between fingers and thumb?

planting botanical shapes in your dreams

Who sculpts the pecan
What forms the hornet's nest
Where is the frog dancing on yonder pond?

Sunbathing turtles share a soul with the artist

Falling

A crescent moon
lay down on a mountainside.
She was tired of the sky.

Partial moons can be hard to discern.

Soft earth made a bed, just fine
for a lounging lunar.
Her long hair streamed down, below ground

forming rivers of silver, gray, and white
beneath her halo of light.
Iguazu and Niagara envied her.

Sunrise in lands to the west
stole light from her mountain crest
and tears fell like oceans in the darkness.

Ages later, when she finally could speak,
Clouds formed from her lips
A vaporous tongue still unknown.

All of this beauty
All her drama
In the silence of twilight.

When looking out a window in the coffee shop

The sidewalk
is littered with socks
dozens undarned
none matching
Pink, purple
white and black
at a bus stop
On E Street.
They warm the concrete,
cobblestone,
And steel grate.

Who loses so many socks
stochastically on a shady street
on a Monday morning?

A puzzlemaster
Someone disabled
A person desperate
for a mate.

Owners

House Mountain glowers
    hulking and towering
Tonight through our window
    that faces the west.

Someone's meadow green and golden
    quilted by spring's sun and shade
Has lain fallow for some time
    Patches sewn together somehow.

Bluebirds, falcons, and deer
    are free over there
But the little country road to get there
    is not free.

On a Sao Paolo Street

Scribbling tiny digits
All day
the transitory transactions
of a store clerk;
Grocery lists, and;
Grounds for divorce;
Call someone back;
Who owes who?
Or is it whom?
A doodle of her day

This pen with a pale pink cap
she thrusts with both arms raised
Above and behind dark black hair
To form a hair bun
made more beautiful
with pen and ink

Athenian Summer

Heat is a divining rod
searching to discover
bodies bathed with moisture
produced from the hot breath
of a universe that howls
as we hug the shade of sidewalks
where we hope to find
truth
among the temples and tchotchke stands.

Camus knew the absurdity of heat.
Serafides lost his bearings in the agony of the day.
Miller wrote of its overpowering nature.

The gods thirst for our sweat
along the hills of the Saronic Gulf

They are omniscient.
They never forget.
our nearly accomplished dreams

Athens Then and Now

Philosophers in flowing white robes
their beards and far-off gazes
all gone but the marble smoothed by their pacing

The lyric poets no longer sing
in odeons of stone still standing
their words chiseled long before Christ.

Even monasteries and mosques
are sealed shut, silent
perfect backdrops for smiling selfies

Manuscripts are no longer
in circulation within
the ruins of Hadrian's library

Today the newsstands no longer
sell the news
only candies and cartoons

As politicians announce at election
something sounding like policies
from car speakers moving at the speed of traffic

Long-thundering Zeus
controls our outcome
and we live like cattle

+++

In the woods outside Socrates's prison
a tour guide lectures young men
"We are the experiments of the gods."

Just then rain chases us from
the hills of Phillipou
to the shelter of an abandoned church

Now the gods can gather alone in peace
to discuss how much longer
this can go on

+++

Everyone can trace
some aspect of their life to this place
of tragedies and comedies

Our bones remember
the azure breezes
that blend this babel of tongues

Return to Sender

There is money in the market
    only not very much

Its hot tin roof and dirty floors
    Where merchants pray to break even

Another shipment came last night
    from the north, always the north

The sellers are yelling at me:

"clothes, clothes, clothes.
    good morning, good morning"

They do not know the schoolgirl.

All she needs is a suitable bag
    to carry books to and from home

Outside the door are plastic-wrapped bailfuls
    of "donated" things from the rich countries far away

Surely among this sea of stuff
    something can carry her dreams

yet the floors are piled high
    with t-shirts and skirts

nikecalvinkleinralphlaurenaddidasarmanikarllagerfeldhanes
fruitoftheloomdkny

There in their midst she finds
    a backpack like those on TV

On her back it fits, if she cinches the ties,
    stitched into the fabric is a strange name

Ashley Shields

So she wears Ashley Shields each day on her back
    to and from school, to and from home.

Maybe she'll write a penpal letter
    she might say

Thank you?
    The question mark is very important.

A streetcar named A.I.

Vacant, no driver,
on Zang Boulevard
a Dallas streetcar
slithers it's way
to a future
no one knows,
because no one
exists anymore

Off High Streets and Main Streets
languages murmured, babbled, uttered, and stuttered
are remembered only by the GPUs
in the cloud, and the old trees still standing

Who's writing this, anyway?

Carolina

Once abundant
still verdant
rows of bright leaf
tobacco grow
along the blacktop
near a Tar Heel grove
Does the farmer know
his crop has blown
from his trailer narrow?
each leaf the size of a crow
His tiny tobacco bin
seemed wider back then.
Behind today's trucks
it looks particularly thin
On its way to dry smokes
in new-fangled barns.
The taxmen try to kill
carcinogens
and the preachers declare it a sin
but it still puts food on the table
for kin and for him.

Ars Poetica

Poetry is the memory, the sadness and humor, despair and hope within me. Places stir these feelings—an airplane seat, an interstate highway, a cold urban street, an enveloping forest, a warm bed. My trajectory in these places often begins with sadness or awe and progresses to humor and hope. I think that is poetry.

About the Author

Following stints working in grocery stores and on petroleum tank farms, Greg Shaw worked as a newspaper reporter in his home state of Oklahoma before going on to government and corporate speechwriting. He's authored, co-authored, and ghostwritten several bestselling nonfiction books. He founded Clyde Hill Publishing, which focuses on technology, and co-founded Pulley Press, a poetry imprint. This is his first collection of poetry.